Kites

By Cameron Macintosh

If you like to be outside,
you could get a kite.

It is fun to have a kite!

Mike has a red kite.

Mine is a white kite.

Nate has a kite that looks like a box.

It has flat sides and stripes.

Trent likes to make kites.

He made this red kite
with his dad.
It is a good size!

Jade has a wide kite.

It can rise up and up!

Kade hikes up a big hill with his kite.

Tug on the line, Kade!

You can win a prize with a kite!

You must make it dive and swish.

This kite looks like a whale.

It is quite a big size!

You can have a good time with a kite!

CHECKING FOR MEANING

1. What is Nate's kite like? *(Literal)*
2. What must you do with a kite to win a prize? *(Literal)*
3. How do you think Trent feels about his kite? *(Inferential)*

EXTENDING VOCABULARY

kite	Look at the word *kite*. What are the sounds in this word? What word can you make if you change the letter *k* to the letter *b*?
white	Say the word *white* slowly. How many sounds are in the word? What words can you think of that rhyme with *white*?
dive	What does the word *dive* mean in the text? What does a kite do if it dives?

MOVING BEYOND THE TEXT

1. What might you need to make a kite?
2. How do kites get up in the air? What is the best weather for flying kites?
3. Which is your favourite kite in the book? Why?
4. What are some other things that can fly in the air?

TIME TO WRITE

Write about the kind of kite you would like to fly and where you would fly it.

PRACTICE WORDS